Joseph Henry Stephenson

Songs of Somerset

Joseph Henry Stephenson

Songs of Somerset

ISBN/EAN: 9783744776257

Printed in Europe, USA, Canada, Australia, Japan

Cover: Foto ©Thomas Meinert / pixelio.de

More available books at **www.hansebooks.com**

Songs of Somerset
by Joseph Henry Stephenson, M.A.

*Rector of Lympsham, and Treasurer
and Prebendary of Wells Cathedral.*

Taunton : Printed and Published by Barnicott & Pearce, Athenæum Press, 44, Fore Street. mdcccxcviii.

In Grateful Memory
of much cordial kindness manifested
to my beloved Wife during earlier years in Hampshire,
and of the unbroken friendship
and boundless hospitality extended to us both at the
Palace of Wells
for a quarter of a century,
this volume
endeavouring to depict some of the scenes she loved
in her adopted County of Somerset
is by her Ladyship's obliging permission
inscribed to
Lady Arthur Hervey
by her faithful friend and servant
Joseph Henry Stephenson.

Preface.

THERE is a wonderful diversity between all our fifty-two English and Welsh counties. Many, indeed, may have their analogies, but each has its own special idiosyncrasies.

This is nowhere truer than in Somerset. Our landscapes, except in the western district, may not rival the glories of our more beautiful sister; but Devon is less "chiselled-out" than Somerset, and has not the variety of hills and plains. Except on Haldon and Dartmoor, you fail to find such extensive and almost panoramic prospects as those that charm your eye from Dundry, Mendip, Quantock, Brendon, Blackdown, and Dunkery.

Some of these I have in this unpretending volume attempted to portray.

I have personally visited all of our British counties, and all but two of those in the Scottish department of our United Kingdom, but nowhere have I found brighter or lovelier scenery than in my native county. We cannot measure beauty by dimension. I remember to have heard a tasteful tourist say of Cheddar Cliffs, "When I saw them first, I admired them greatly, but then I had seen nothing : now, I have been everywhere, and have seen everything, and have come back to admire them more than ever !"

Many of the following poems have appeared in volumes which have long been out of print.

Lympsham Manor,
April, 1898.

Contents.

	Page
Preface	vii
Our Somerset Churches	1
Willett Tor	8
Dunkery	10
Culbone	15
Quantock	21
Egremont Inn at Williton	23
Adieus from Mendip	25
Autumn Lights on my Native Hills	28
Friends in Familiar Objects	30
Crook's Peak	32
Away to the Quantocks	35
Shadows on Mendip	36
Wells from Mendip	38

Contents

I've seen the Wild Hielands	40
The Grange Walk at Lympsham	42
Mendip on an Autumn Morning	44
To the Clump of Scotch Firs on Bleadon Hill	45
A Brean Down Parable	46
Suggested by Passing the Glastonbury Churchyard	49
Marriage of H.R.H. The Prince of Wales	50
Morning after a Hurricane	52
A Morning Walk on the Severn Shore	55
Home, Sweet Home	57
To my Lympsham Bells	60
The Kilve Shore	62
Brent Knoll	64
The Brean Down Cloud	79
Autumn	81
The Firs have Fallen	83
Buncombe Hill on a Summer's Evening	84
Greenaleigh	86
The Glastonbury Gathering	88
Early Snow in Autumn	90
Easter Even	94
Christmas	96

Contents.

xi

Pleasure and Duty . .	101
I Pace the Ocean's Rugged Shore	103
Falling Bells .	105
Wordsworth's Grave .	108
The Bee Hive .	112
Appendix .	113

Songs of Somerset.

Our Somerset Churches.

'TIS Christmas Eve! and thoughts that burn
In quick succession each return;
And soon the spell is woven round
Wherein my waiting soul is bound.
Yet once again this Christmas joy,
Unchecked and boundless in the boy,
Looks in e'en still upon the man,
Though life has well-nigh reached its span.
Fond memory turns tow'rds scenes long past,
As setting suns their radiance cast
O'er long-left plain and distant hill,
Where beams of even linger still.
Such recollections in me wake
Whene'er towards Wells my course I take,

And stand beneath the minster fair,
Counting each saint depicted there ;
In stone without, in glass meanwhile,
In storied pane, through long-drawn aisle.
The charm of infantine surprise,
When first these glories met mine eyes—
Led blindfold by a father's hand,
Bidden by him where first to stand,
And then with lifted lids survey
This wondrous church on summer day—
In loved retention may not part
From the recesses of my heart !
No fane in Albion's length outvies
The features which our church supplies,
When Cynthia flings her silver light
O'er the grey pile in silent night ;
Or when meridian rays aspire
To gild the arches of our choir ;
When pillar, niche, and cusped recess
Stand forth the golden beam to bless,
And melodies come stealing o'er
The soul, well-nigh entranced before.
If peace on sin-struck earth might dwell,
And build below her tranquil cell,

Surely beneath yon drawbridge tower
She would select her secret bower
Where softly sleeps the guardian moat,
Where snow-winged swans in silence float,
And lawn, and shrub, and bright parterre
Combine within the pleasaunce fair.
In larger cities of our land,
Where still our grand cathedrals stand,
The church seems lost 'mid smoke and din,
Hidden decaying walls within ;
But here the *town* forgotten lies,
As triple towers arrest the eyes ;
And proud St. Andrew's sacred fane
O'er the whole scene is felt to reign ;
While house, and hall, and close, and street
Seem to do homage at his feet.
Mark where yon shapely knoll on high
Lifts brave St. Michael to the sky,
With ruined abbey 'neath the crest,
Once the chief glory of the West,
From good King Ina's distant reign
The wonder of the verdant plain,
Till Henry's sacrilegious hand
The Church despoiled throughout the land.

Here, ages back, the pilgrim came,
Who bore St. Joseph's noble name,
Whose magic staff has blossoms borne
Since with his comrades, spent and worn,
He rested on the grassy hill
Whose name records the legend still,
And, as the shades of evening fall,
Proclaims itself as "Weary-all."
Few towers in Somerset outvie,
In stateliness and symmetry,
That which St. John doth patron claim,
A shrine well worthy of his name.
O Somerset! thy lordly fanes,
So thickly scattered o'er thy plains,
May rival well the structures tall
Through England's counties one and all.
Norfolk and Suffolk proudly boast
Of goodly churches down their coast;
Northampton, Lincoln, both acquire
Their well-won palm for soaring spire;
But neither region stands possessed
Of *towers* like those within the West.
Go, traveller, to Taunton, Wells,
To Evercreech, and Leigh, and Mells,

To Bruton, Petherton, Fitzpaine,
To Hewish, Kingsbury on the plain ;
To Chewton, Winscombe, where the hill
Gives grander elevation still ;
To Backwell, Wraxall, Dundry high,
Piercing with pinnacles the sky ;
To Zoyland, Lympsham, Lydeard, Lyng ;
To Banwell, Cheddar, where the spring
Flows from each rock, like Horeb's stream,
And sparkles in the summer beam ;
To Kilmersdon, amongst them all,
To Portishead, so stern and tall ;
To Abbots Isle, and Kingston, too,
Proceed ere closing thy review ;
And Wellington, whose noble name
Entwines itself with Albion's fame ;
Keynsham and Batcombe pass not by
Should they within your circuit lie ;
But last, not least, with joy survey—
A sight to last full many a day—
Wrington, by architects confessed
Of all his compeers first and best !
Devon, in grove and sylvan glen,
Hides her meek sanctuaries from men,

Who here and there delighted see
Some tower 'neath verdant canopy ;
But Somerset her fanes displays,
To meet the wondering tourist's gaze,
On hill, in dale ; through plains abroad
Rise the grand temples of our God !
No Christmas Eve, or opening year,
Can in these western climes appear
Unwelcomed by the steeple's voice,
That would responsively rejoice
At break of day, when changes ring
Glad greetings to the newborn King.
And shall these structures perish all ?
These bells be still, these steeples fall ?
And reckless hand of rude decay
Tear their proud minarets away ?
Shall sanctuaries forsaken lie,
And rifled roofs reveal the sky ?
Shall school and parsonage disappear,
With summer treat and Christmas cheer ?
And pastor's voice no longer bless
The pastures of the wilderness ?
The lady's hand no healing bring,
Causing the widow's heart to sing ?

Shall hungry pauper cease to share
With parson's family their fare?
And loving little ones no more
Bring the full basket to the door?
Say: shall torn shrub and untrimmed bower
Tell of a brighter bygone hour?
And warbling note of spring-tide song
No more its melody prolong?
Forbid it, Heaven ! My country rise !
Rend off the veil that blinds thine eyes ;
Let not Philistia's envious band
Despoil the strength of Samson's hand,
Nor Liberation's treacherous sway
Lead the proud Nazarite away !

Willett Tor.[1]

THE mountain pines are sighing,
    On Willett's lonely height;
The landscape round is lying,
    All bathed in golden light.

Before us, Quantock rises,
    Still queen of all around;
Each wondering eye surprises
    With her enchanted ground.

Behind us, Brendon swelling,
    Her widening fields displays;
Beneath, her knolls are telling
    Of spring's returning days.

Below, fair Lydeard sleepeth,
    Her verdant meads among :
And sweet Combe Florey peepeth
    Forth from her groves of song.

There's Cothelstone and Hartrow,
    And many a lordly seat :

[1] *See* APPENDIX, Note 1.

Gay Crowcombe and blithe Bagbro'
    Shine smiling at our feet!

Yonder the silvery ocean
    Fringes the cliff-bound strand,
With scarce a wave in motion
    'Twixt this and Cambria's land.

O God of beauteous nature,
    Thy glorious works we praise:
From creature to Creator,
    Our raptured thoughts we raise.

Dunkery[1]

From my Shrubbery Walk at Lympsham.

YON mountain grey,
   Lies miles away,
   'Mid moorland and 'mid heather :
  Seen dim or clear,
  Far off or near,
He tells the coming weather.

  I've climbed his crest,
  Where mist-wreaths rest,
Alternate bright and darkling ;
  As storm awoke,
  Or sunbeam broke,
Around the Beacon sparkling.

  So still and lone,
  Upsoared his cone,
'Mid streams from Exe's fountain ;
  The desert's king,
  He seemed to fling
His sceptre o'er the mountain.

[1] *See* APPENDIX, Note 2.

From base to crest,
His sides were drest,
In purple heath, wide waving;
And whortle wild,
The "mountain's child,"
The morning dews were laving.

Deep in his side,
In virgin pride,
Young oak and birch lay sleeping;
And down the glen,
The ear might ken,
The gurgling streamlet leaping.

His foot below,
In ebb and flow,
The blue-wave crests were gleaming;
And pebbly beach,
Round every reach,
A silver border seeming.

In dales between,
From woodland screen,
The modest towers were peeping;

And hamlets fair,
Lay here and there,
All up the hill-sides creeping.

On this side Wales,
Her heights and vales
In landscape soft was lending;
On this, upsprung
The clouds among,
The Dartmoor peaks ascending.

Here Malvern high,[1]
Assails the sky,
With Bredon's summit hoary;
And Mendip blue,
And Cotswold too,
Add each their share of glory.

And nearer still,
Lie Brendon Hill
And Croydon range, his brother;
This clear and bare,
With forehead fair,
With heath-capt brow the other.

[1] This may be a little poetical licence.

Here Exmoor wide
May be descried,
His dingy downs outspreading;
With many a steed,
Of mountain breed,
The countless acres treading.

No beacon bright
Gleams now at night,
Its war-behest displaying;
Yet as of yore
Are hearthstones four,
And furnaces decaying.

The warrior's dust,
In sacred trust,
The craggy crest defendeth;
And shrill sea mew,
And wild curlew,
Their notes for requiem lendeth.

Dunkery, adieu!
'Twixt me and you
Strange sympathy ariseth:

The heart's desire
Thy wilds inspire,
My wondering friend surpriseth !

But few there are,
Or near or far,
Who taste the hidden pleasures
That Nature lends
To him who bends
Meek thought upon her treasures.

Then farewell still,
Immortal hill,
My friend and chosen brother :
Till time her drooping wing shall fold,
Mysterious converse will we hold,
Deep meanings tell each other !

Culbone.[1]

After the manner of Scott.

THE slanting beams of closing day,
Gleamed golden o'er our westward way;
As ravished with prolonged delight
We left the mountain's cloud-capt height,
Where, lingering through the summer hours,
Amid the heather's purple flowers,
Enchanted by the landscape's spell,
We gazed on grove, and gorge, and fell!
And now, just verging on the deep,
Like infant soft in cradled sleep,
A peaceful hamlet smiling lay,
Reposing in its pebbly bay.
To guard each fishing boat and barge,
Rude hands had piled the fragments large—
Which, crumbling from the crags on high,
In many a rugged mass would lie—
That seaman's hand might bravely steer
His pinnace round the rocky pier,
Where, anchored safely and at rest,

[1] *See* APPENDIX, Note 3.

She might dance gaily on the breast
Of rippling wave, which soft and slow
Came eddying round her heaving prow.
The village hostel might you see
Uprising from the rustic quay;
And at its portal, trimly drest,
Mine hostess to invite her guest,
And point the way up oaken stair,
To tourist or to lady fair.
Without—the myrtle and the vine
Their varying hues and scents combine;
Within—the generous walls afford
Sleep, shelter, and a frugal board.
Behind the house, the matron's care
Had decked each border and parterre
With hardier plants, which blossomed free,
Despite the vapours of the sea,
And western gale that oft would sweep,
Athwart the salt waves of the deep.
The garden crossed, a pathway leads
Through waving corn and fragrant meads,
Which, sloping 'neath the neighbouring height
The shingles with the cliffs unite.
A sylvan farm now greets the view,

With cattle-shed and straw-yard too,
And just above, on terraced height,
Ashley-Combe Lodge appears in sight,
With ivied walls, fantastic deckt,
With battlement and minaret,
Art of Italian architect.
Pass we with silent step the door,
O'er velvet turf that slopes before ;
Then plunge into yon tangled screen
The fair domain and cliffs between ;
Tread yonder bank, " with footing nice "
By the o'erhanging precipice,
Where oak and mountain ash on high
Have weaved their verdant canopy.
Along the cliff we wend our way,
Which skirts the margin of the bay ;
Now through luxuriant copse-wood led,
Now winding round the rocky head,
Two lonely miles the path proceeds,
Resistless in enchantment leads
To a green patch of forest glade,
Emerging from the coppice shade ;
The heath-clad hill swells round and bold,

And blends with Exmoor's desert wold ;
Till, soaring to the bending sky,
It blazes in the beams on high,
Which visit rare the dale below,
Where winding cliffs shut out the glow,
And change the summer hues so bright,
To watery winter's paler light !
Leaping from off the lichened rock,
Deep rifted by the lightning's shock,
The brooklet brown hoarse murmurs past ;
Now lost to sight, now widening fast,
Till down the gorge our feet beside,
It mingles with old ocean's tide.
Soft sheltered in this lonely glen,
So distant from the haunts of men,
The modest spirelet points to Heaven,
And, when each blest first day of seven
Gladdens the weary peasant's bower,
Steals the gay chime from tiny tower,
Till valley soft, and splintered fell
Are echoing back the Sabbath bell.
No " storied window richly dight "
Greets antiquary's ravished sight,

But gothic mullion sharp and true,
Gable and buttress may you view,
And oaken bench and rough rood screen,
The altar and the nave between.
Without—the cross seems watch to keep
O'er villagers who round it sleep ;
And yew, that furnished many a bow,
Sighs drooping o'er the bowmen low.
The hamlet fair has passed away :
Yet linger still, despite decay,
Two smiling cots in village pride,
With garden-patch around supplied ;
And higher up the opening glade,
'Mong widening meads, and rarer shade,
The homesteads with low barn and byre,
'Mid walls of mossy stone retire ;
Where fleecy flocks the slopes adorn,
And huntsman winds his bugle horn.
 But cease my strain ! This rustic lay
I weave for love of thee, dear Grey ;
For ne'er shall Culbone's wilds arise,
In golden tints to memory's eyes,
But thoughts of him shall with them glide,

Who walked fraternal at my side,
When last our Highland steeps I viewed,
Majestic in their solitude ;
And knoll, and rill, and glen and grove,
Shall each recall a brother's love !

Quantock[1]

From my Study Window.

QUANTOCK, as I gaze on thee
Bounds my heart with ecstacy!
Now the darkling shadows sleep,
Now the sparkling sunbeams leap,
Now thy slopes resplendent gleam,
Now thy valleys slumbering seem,
Now so near 'neath clouds on high,
Now so far 'neath azure sky.
I have gashed the lordly tree,
Quantock, to make room for thee;
Gothic arch of leaflets light,
Frames the picture blue and bright.
Burnham's lighthouse in the plain,
Rises silvery from the main,
Backed by Aisholt's heathery glen,
Crowned by Bagborough's heights again.
Roams my fancy, while I stand,
Through thy groves, dear Quantock land;

[1] *See* APPENDIX, Note 4.

Where the brooks glide murmuring on,
Twinkling in the noontide sun :
Where the aromatic air,
Charms away fatigue and care,
Where the landscapes rich supply
Gorgeous canvas for the eye.
Where sweet Nature tints hath twined,
Purple, golden, green combined :
Woodland, ocean, dark morass,
Jutting crag and hollow pass :
Cultured slope, and wild forlorn,
Heather blue and yellow corn.
From my turret oft I trace
Smiling welcomes in thy face,
Looking through the leafy screen,
Where my elms are gashed between.

Egremont Inn, at Williton.

1856.

TILL smiles the welcome in the village inn,
    Still swings the sign before the well-known
        door:
I fly from busy scenes of dust and din,
    To seek repose, where frequent found before.

Once with a parent, passed into his rest,
    Twice with a partner dear as life to me,
Often with friends and kind companions blest,
    Sometimes alone, fair inn, I've entered thee.

The morrow's dawn must break my slumbers light,
    The mountain heather waits my joyous tread;
Yonder the heath bell and the gorse so bright,
    On the lone hillsides lie all richly spread.

I go to quaff a draught of mountain air:
    I go to gaze on loveliness below:
I go to meet the God of nature there,
    Where cliffs are climbing, and where brooklets flow.

I go to bathe my jaded spirit weary,
   Within the soft, the beautiful, the wild :
I go to solitudes that men call dreary,
   But 'mid whose stillness I'm again a child !

Lord of creation, meet me on the mountain :
   Smile in each valley, speak from crag and tree !
My spirit may not drink the living fountain,
   Save in Thy works, my God, I witness Thee.

Adieus from Mendip,

On leaving home for a temporary absence.

On Mendip's brow I turned me round,
    To sigh a last adieu,
To trees, and streams, and dales, and downs,
    Fast fading from my view.

Good-bye, old Bleadon, just below,
    Snug in thy sheltering glade;
Thy tower looks sadly, while I go,
    All sombre in the shade.

Good-bye, Brent Knoll, with silver spire,
    Heaven-pointing 'neath thy crest.
Thou peerless diamond of our shire,
    Thou emerald of the west.

Good-bye, fair Burnham, Berrow, Brean,
    With lighthouse, shore, and Down,
Good-bye, ye islets, grey or green
    As ye or smile or frown.

Good-bye, dear Quantock, bold and blue,
  And Dunkery 'neath the sky,
With Brendon, Croydon, Grabhurst, too,
  Porlock, and Greenaleigh.

Good-bye, soft Polden's lengthy line,
  So modest in thy rise,
Where elm, and oak, and darkling pine,
  Ravish the gazer's eyes.

Good-bye, famed Glaston's sacred Tor,
  And Montacute behind,
With Badgworth, Nyland, and Wedmōre,
  And Weare's green slopes combined.

And last not least, my cherished home,
  My old grey tower, good-bye:
Where'er through this wide earth I roam,
  Thou shalt not leave mine eye!

For memory's glance, so keen and clear,
  Shall fondly turn to thee;
To childhood, youth, and manhood dear,
  In sorrow and in glee.

Wrapt in thy vest of ancient shade,
　　The glory of the plain,
I shall not see a goodlier glade,
　　Till I see thine again.

I dashed away the dimming haze,
　　That welled around mine eye,
Nor suffered it again to gaze,
　　With this, my last good-bye.

Autumn Lights on my Native Hills.

THE richest glow of autumn's red
    On swelling Mendip lay,
  And Cheddar's rocks, with glistening head,
Flung back their roseate ray.

No storm disturbed the gentle scene,
  So calm the valleys slept;
You might have thought the whole had been
  By painter's pencil swept.

How soothing is the beautiful,
  'Mid turmoil, and 'mid strife,
If with a spirit dutiful,
  Man will but taste her life.

It is not sensuous pleasure
  That charms my ravished eye;
'Tis richer, costlier treasure
  That beauty doth supply.

I converse with creation
  Daily delight to hold;

Full many a sweet sensation,
    Glows from her mine of gold.

These mountains are my brothers,
    Yon swelling Knoll my friend ;
Hours glide, like time with lovers,
    That we together spend !

My human friends may fail me,
    Stern death may lay them low ;
But let the worst assail me,
    These loved ones cannot go.

Sweet Quantock, and dear Mendip,
    I'll gaze my last on you,
Till pulses of fond friendship,
    Shall sink in death still true.

Then let your gorse and heather,
    Weave my bier's coronal :
Thy fern my hearse's feather,
    Thy sedge my funeral pall !

Friends in Familiar Objects.

THOUGH friends be gone and hopes be fled,
And loved ones numbered with the dead;
Still, as I view each cherished scene,
I cannot lack dear friends, I ween.

Still giant Mendip rises fair,
And cliff, and crag, and peak are there;
Still widening Severn's silver band,
Links our loved coast to Cambria's land.

Still queenly Quantock soareth high,
And Dunkery leaning on the sky;
And lowly Polden gently swells,
With grassy slopes and elm-clad dells.

Still the grey tower smiles as of yore,
'Mid weather-stains and lichen hoar;
And vocal clock, and soothing chime,
Cheat memory of the lapse of time.

Still elm, and oak, and laurel screen,
Are yet, as they have ever been;

And shrubbery soft, and summer flowers,
Smile as in childhood's careless hours.

O tower, and trees, and hills, with ye
I cannot solitary be :
While ye your soothing influence lend,
I cannot be without a friend !

Crook's Peak.

BORDERED beneath by emerald plain,
　　Wide stretching westward to the main,
　　　　Thou flinty peak arise :
And with thy kindred heights around,
Scorn trees and towers on humbler ground,
　　　　And lift thee to the skies !

Within the crags that form thy crest
The mountain swallow builds her nest,
　　　　While storm comes howling past :
And winter snow-clouds silent fall,
Weaving their silvery virgin pall,
　　　　Over thy slopes to cast.

Bleak desolation yonder reigns,
As turn we from the southern plains,
　　　　Where sunbeams glow and smile :
And far 'mid Mendip's forest lone
We gaze o'er sedge and " cold grey stone "
　　　　For many a dreary mile.

One soft green patch you yet may trace
On the bluff mountain's furrowed face,
    Inviting us to climb :
'Tis where yon aged stunted yew
Looks out upon us, fresh and true,
    As friend of olden time!

Embosomed in its leafy glade,
Beneath the hill's protecting shade,
    In gentle contrast sleeps
Yon peaceful hamlet, coy and meek,
Like modesty with blushing cheek,
    That in retirement keeps.

Never a Sabbath morn appears
Through the long course of changeful years,
    Over yon eastern trees,
But you may hear each tuneful bell
In varying cadence sink and swell,
    Borne on the balmy breeze.

Hail modest manse, and lichened tower!
Hail village green, and garden bower,
    And school-house just below ;

And homesteads scattered here and there,
'Mid copse-wood gay and pasture fair!
   I linger as I go.

Away to the Quantocks.

AWAY to the Quantocks, come wander with me,
As fleet as the wild deer, as blithe as the bee:
The heather is blooming on Cothelstone's crest,
The bracken is waving o'er Bagborough's breast;
The dingles of Aisholt are verdant and gay,
Nor Autumn's fell finger hath seared e'en a spray;
And Ely's bright brooklets are sparkling along,
Meandering so bonnie 'mid sunshine and song.

No monarch stands prouder in purple and gold,
'Mid courtiers all countless and cohorts untold,
Than we shall this noontide on Wills-neck's fair height,
'Mid gorse and 'mid heath-bell so blue and so bright!
Then point not to Devon, and boast not to me,
Our famed southern sister a rival is she:
A brave three-times-three for our county we'll raise,
As "Garden of England," we'll Somerset praise!

Shadows on Mendip.

THE skies that true poets love
    Are not of your cloudless blue;
But the storm-streaked fields above,
    With colours of every hue.

We love not the dimming haze
    That waits on the summer's ray:
We love on those wreaths to gaze,
    That are passing the desert's way.

For now they are giant towers,
    All battle-despoiled and riven;
And now they are angel-bowers,
    Or silvery steps to Heaven.

We love not unbroken brightness,
    Outpoured on the mountain's breast:
We love the ascending whiteness,
    That shews but his peering crest.

For Mystery reigns in the vapours,
   Enshrined on her throne unseen ;
And gleams through storms are her tapers,
   To flash us a glimpse within !

Wells from Mendip

December, 1858.

After the manner of Scott.

SEEK I for beauties rich and rare?
  Scarce may I find a scene more fair,
    'Mid valley or 'mid down,
Than greets the eye from Mendip bold,
Where first thy features I behold,
    "Mine own romantic town!"

There's Glaston, lifting straight on high
Brave old St. Michael to the sky,
    'Mid sunshine and 'mid storm;
With many a terraced height beneath,
Now clear, now wrapt in misty wreath,
    In strange fantastic form.

Ashcot, and Montacute, and Brent,
Pennard, and distant hills of Trent,
    With Quantock blue behind;

Blagdon, and Brendon, Dunkery too,
Crowding the panoramic view
 Of hill and dale combined.

Then come thy minster's massy towers,
Rising from out the trees and bowers
 That here spontaneous rise :
And cloistered halls and ruins grey
Sleep in the shade of parting day,
 As fail these wintry hours !

I've Seen the Wild Hielands.

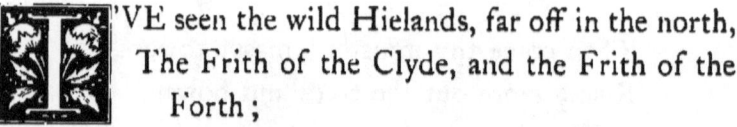'VE seen the wild Hielands, far off in the north,
The Frith of the Clyde, and the Frith of the Forth;
But there's nought in mine eye like my ain cliff and sea:
The brave Bristol Channel and Mendip for me!

I've climbed up Ben Lomond, cloud-capped in the air,
I've sailed down Loch Katrine, enchantingly fair,
I've marked the bright Tweed, rushing forth to be free;
But there's nought like the Exe and old Dunkery for
    me!

Loch Ard, and Loch Arklet, and sweet Loch Achray,
Loch Lomond's green islets have gladdened my way,
The Eden-like Trosachs and Vennachar's lea;
But there's nought like the dingles of Quantock for me!

Loch Lubnaig's sweet copses and Tay's verdant side,
Dunkeld in her beauty, and Blair in her pride—
All these in succession have mine been to see;
But there's nought like the woodlands of Loxton for me!

The Cheviots, and Eildons, and Pentlands so blue,
The Grampians have burst on my ravishèd view,
And Arthur's high Seat looking forth o'er the sea ;
But there's nought like the Knoll or the old " Crook "
    for me!

The Grange Walk at Lympsham.

A Summer Evening's Stroll.

EMERGING from the closer shade,
   By frequent trees so densely made,
   I love to wander fresh and free
Up the green sward of broader lea !

To catch the breeze of sea-borne air,
To gaze upon the summits fair,
That north, south, east, and westward rise,
Attractive to their kindred skies.

Here swells the Knoll with modest head,
With emerald mantle overspread,
And silver spire 'mid elms below,
And woodlands as you upward go.

Behind us soars the statelier crest
Of the grey " Crook " in silent rest,
With steepy side of limestone blue,
Piercing the grassy covering through.

Yonder's the undulating down,
Breasting the Severn's waters brown,
That bids the outward-bound adieu,
And welcomes each returning crew.

Quantock is stretching far away,
Where sinks the sun's declining ray,
And Dunkery with his triple cone
Looms lofty from his desert lone.

O, Somerset ! thy hills and plains,
Dear as the life blood of my veins,
Linked with the shades of days gone by,
The very apple of mine eye,

No fleeting years which change must see,
Shall ever witness change in me,
Thy worthless but most constant son,
Till life her latest course hath run !

Mendip, on an Autumn Morning.

F thou would'st view stern Mendip best,
    Go when the mist steals o'er its breast:
    Go while autumnal tints are gay,
Ere the seared leaf has passed away.
Go while the slopes are crimsoned o'er,
Ere yet the rugged heights are hoar :
Go ere the flakes of wintry snow
Have veiled the verdant plain below.
Go when the sunbeam from the cloud
Streaks the grey Crook " with lustre proud,"
And, gently gliding from its crest,
Bids Compton smile beneath its breast,
Then, following up the mist-wreath's way,
Gilds Cheddar with departing ray !

To the Clump of Scotch Firs on Bleadon Hill.

STATELY and still, on Mendip's brow ye rise,
Wet with the mist-wreath darkling as it flies,
Sparkling all gaily through the summer shower,
Silvered with snowflakes in the wintry hour,
Moaning so sadly 'mid the autumn's wail,
Whisp'ring so softly in the springtide gale!

A Breane Down Parable.

INDENTED on a rocky ledge
    A shallow basin lay,
Reflecting from its rugged edge
    The cliffs that closed the bay.

I marked beneath the radiant west,
    The glistening waters swim;
Till swelling waves with golden crest
    Rose to that basin's brim.

They mingled with that melting blue,
    Convulsed the mirror's face;
And jets of living diamonds flew
    Forth from their wild embrace.

No longer did the lakelet still
    Give back the mountain's form;
But you might mark proud breakers fill
    And lash its calm to storm.

Meanwhile, I wandered to-and-fro
  Along the sounding shore ;
Then said, " 'Methinks before I go
  I'll see this pool once more."

The tide had sunk beneath the ledge,
  For hours had passed away ;
And once again the glassy edge
  Reflected the fair bay.

Breakers no more tossed high their surge,
  But, bending low, retired ;
The wave that kissed the lakelet's verge
  Sighed gently and expired.

Still, as I gazed, that pool to me
  A parable supplied ;
Each stage of man I seemed to see
  Before my vision glide.

In early childhood, calm and blest,
  The lake of life doth sleep ;
And, dancing on its quivering breast,
  Youth's softest shadows keep.

But passion's rising surf at length
    Comes swelling to the shore ;
And billows, in resistless strength,
    That tranquil pool explore.

Yet, as the tide of time retires,
    Contending passions cease :
Heaven tranquillizes earth's desires :
    Once more the lake is peace !

Suggested by passing the Glastonbury Churchyard

Now no longer a burial ground, but a garden, since the opening of the new cemetery.

WHEN last I marked the minster grey,
    Within its rood of hallowed ground,
  Full many a hillock round it lay,
And open graves were gaping round.

But now mortality hath flown,
    And sepulchres have disappeared;
Taste hath with flowers the graveyard strewn,
    And many a smiling shrub hath reared.

How sweet the emblem! Now, within
    Her upheaved yard the church appears:
Death lies around, the curse of sin,
    With tombs, and mourners, graves, and tears.

But in the Resurrection Morn,
    'Mid changeless bays the church shall stand
No more among her graves forlorn,
    But smiling on her risen band!

Marriage of H.R.H. the Prince of Wales
March 10th, 1863.

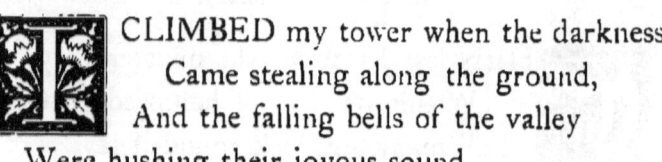CLIMBED my tower when the darkness
    Came stealing along the ground,
And the falling bells of the valley
    Were hushing their joyous sound.

And I gazed around on the prospect,
    All radiant with bonfire glow,
That told of county rejoicings,
    As far as the eye could go.

Old "Crook" was twinkling in twilight,
    And Mendip had caught the flame;
And Worlebury, bright o'er the Channel,
    Had rivalled her ancient fame.

Fair Quantock began to sparkle,
    And Polden opened her eye,
And hoary tower-crowned Glaston
    Gleamed red on the eastern sky.

But of all the enkindled beacons,
    The bonniest of the whole
Was fed by the crackling faggots
    That laughed on our own Brent Knoll.

Morning after a Hurricane.

After the manner of Longfellow.

I HAD opened a rustic window
    Through the boughs of yon stately trees,
That I might catch the mountains
    Across the southern seas.

And oft to my verdant casement
    Those heights would their blue crests bring,
At morn like some blushing maiden,
    At eve like some crownèd king.

And thus did I glimpse the hillsides,
    Within but a tiny span;
Though the eye of imagination
    Away o'er their summits ran.

At length a jealous tornado
    Came straight from those southern seas,
Despoiling the goodly hedgerow,
    And maiming the lordly trees.

And as their gnarlèd branches
    Came crashing about the ground,
I wept like a very infant
    On the ghastly scene around.

But now the hurricane's over,
    And the sky is again serene,
I gaze on the far blue mountains,
    And the emerald dale between.

No longer a single summit,
    Or a soaring crest I see,
Just peeping but through the branches
    Of my long-loved fallen tree.

Quantock herself appeareth,
    With her undulating line :
I have lost my leaf-clad brother,
    But the mountain is yet more mine.

And thus the rude storms of sorrow,
    That our cherished joys lay low,
That strew, with the wrecks that are dearest,
    These earthly abodes of woe,

But open our distant prospects,
  That afar may be seen to rise
Those fair Delectable Mountains
  That lean on eternal skies!

A Morning Walk on the Severn Shore.

WEARY and sad I sought the wave-washed shore,
    And found refreshment for my toil-worn
       brain :
Sweet nature sympathized and brought relief !
I was a very child in joy once more,
Happy as when long since I castle raised,
Or fondly traced upon the level sand
Some much-loved name !   As I approached,
The farther Holm smiled recognition, bright beneath
The ray, and Dunkery, triple-crested, soared on high :
Cambria all grey, through her thin azure veil,
Loomed coyly to my gaze, and then retired ;
While in the foreground the more rocky isle
Looked blue and wan beneath the passing cloud.
At length the mist withdrew, and one by one
Its cliffs all radiant caught the beam and glowed !
And so at last the whole stood forth illum'd,
As if some angel-wing had swept the sky.
Meanwhile, the sinking storm that last night raged,
And tore from forest tree the bending bough,

Soothed, as some infant, softly-cradled, slept ;
And heavenly calm breathed hallowed influence round.
And thus life mirrored rose before my view,
Now cloud portentous, now returning ray,
Now darksome mountain-isle in frowning guise,
Now peaceful haven where the wavelets dance,
Sparkling in diamonds as they kiss the shore.
Lord, give me patience in the ills of life,
And faith to trust Thee with the cloud between !
It will not always blow, nor ever frown,
The Bow of Promise gleams athwart the storm.

Home, Sweet Home.

THERE are who leave their ancient home
  In foreign lands afar to roam,
    And feast their eye 'neath mountain pine
From snowy Alp or Apennine;
To glide beneath the "Bridge of Sighs"
In gondola, where Venice lies;
To view each painting, rich and rare,
In studios of Florence fair;
To wander through Eternal Rome,
And gaze upon Saint Peter's dome;
Or mark where Strasbourg's soaring fane
Lifts to the clouds its topmost vane;
Or ask, "Did skill of sprite or fay
Create thee, beautiful Beauvais?"
Yet be it mine through life to dwell
'Mid cherished scenes remembered well,
Where tower, nor tree, nor glen, nor stone,
Nor sinks, nor soars to me unknown!
When, worn by long-continued toil,
Mine be the rest of Aberfoyle;

In Newark's "beechen bowers" to stray,
Where Ettrick stretches far away;
Helvellyn and Scawfell for me,
Soft Grasmere's vale and Esthwaite's lea,
And Ingleborough's broad incline,
Or Cheviot's undulating line.
Few goodlier Goshen's gazers greet
Than those which lie 'neath Malvern's feet.
No panorama may compare
With Dunkery's prospect high in air.
Give me blue Mendip's arching form,
Whether in sunshine or in storm,
Or Quantock's groves, where angels stray,
Awhile delayed on mercy's way;
For me let Lincoln's booming bell
"Fling o'er the fen its ponderous knell,"
And Chichester and Sarum rise,
Pointing their needles to the skies;
Or thou, old Wells, with triple towers,
Lichened and stained with frequent showers,
Which circling Mendip's heights detain
On their way landward from the main.
Mine be the "Crook," to childhood dear,
With Compton nestling in the rear;

Mine the more modest verdant Knoll,
The spire below, on high the pole ;
And mine the home, two miles away,
Where first these eyes beheld the day ;
And mine the manor, church, and tower,
And wind-stripped elm and summer bower ;
And mine the visions that remain,
And memories that recur again ;
And mine the sacred spell that binds
To life-known scenes accordant minds.
No throstle warbles on the spray,
No blackbird pipes through summer-day,
No cawing rook, or twittering wren
Can sound but childhood comes again,
And intervening periods fade
Like shadows on the mountains laid.
O Recollection ! kindly given
To cheer our pilgrimage to heaven,
'Tis thine the mystic charm to throw
O'er God's objective world below.

To my Lympsham Bells.

ALOFT within my old church tower
   I placed ye, tuneful five:
    Once more the belfry, hour by hour,
With music seems alive.

Your ancient forbears so long hung
   That melody had fled,
Whether some wedding peal were rung,
   Or knell to mourn the dead.

Regenerate now, with melting voice
   Ye woo the swains to pray,
And bid the region round rejoice
   Upon the festal day.

But that a still more perfect stave
   Might from our steeple sound,
A virgin sister-sixth I gave
   To swell the gladsome round.

Yet, when this new-born sister came,
    Her voice sang strange and shrill :
The note was clear, the key the same,
    Far from accordant still !

But when the tuner's magic hand
    Two hours had worked one day,
It seemed as if at his command
    My Six rolled right away.

Sweetly those sisters, singing true,
    In harmony combined,
When Cynthia shews herself to view
    Fling music on the wind !

The Kilve Shore.

Inscribed to the Rev. Hay Sweet-Escott, M.A., Rector of Kilve-cum-Stringston.

IF peace I seek, oppressed with strife,
    Or solace midst surrounding care,
    Or respite from the toils of life,
Where shall I find them?—tell me where!

Follow the rivulet that flows
    Down Kilve's green valley to the sea :
Its very murmur breathes repose,
    Its every wave is melody.

No angry billows surge the main,
    No tempest's voice is heard to roar :
The Channel seems one crystal plain,
    'Twixt this and yonder Cambrian shore !

The fleecy cloud is stealing slow
    O'er queenly Quantock's swelling side ;
Now cradled in the combe below,
    Now stretching o'er the mountain wide.

The modest belfry hides its head
    The ivied priory beside :
Around it sleep the silent dead,
    Who the Archangel's trump abide.

I wonder not that Wordsworth found
    Sweet solace in this soft retreat,
Where hospitalities abound,
    And cherished friendship's whispers greet.

Escott ! long may thy lot be cast
    Within Kilve's manse, serene and free,
Till thou shalt rise to join at last
    " The minstrels on the glassy sea ! "

Brent Knoll.

This poem requires a few words of explanation. It is a very juvenile production, having been written when the author was a lad of seventeen, on leaving home for a six years' exile, after the death of a beloved father. As it was out of print, and has been asked for, it is again given to the public, but must be read with indulgence.

AONIAN Nymphs, my feeble voice inspire,
    Nerve ye the hand that strikes a rustic lyre!
    And, gentle stranger, kind attention pay,
While I attune my unadornéd lay.
Yon shapely Knoll that greets the traveller's eye
'Swells from the vale' and rises to the sky,
Pleasing in detail, yet august in form,
Called by the mariner—"The Isle of Storm."
Be this my theme, the subject of my song,
While fingers sweep the varying chords along.
What though sad memory tells of beauties flown,
And woodlands fair that by-gone times have known,
Which now, alas, the climber fails to find
On the bare shoulder of the hill reclined;
What though the tower that lately crowned the height
Lies now demolished—buried out of sight;

What though the pine that formed the upland's crest
Has drooped its head and softly sunk to rest;
What though the forest oak no more appears,
Nor from the summit his proud form uprears;
Yet verdure still is found in every glade,
And hazel-nut and tangled copse-wood shade:
Cowslip and primrose still adorn each lea,
And court the visit of the passing bee;
And gurgling brook still trickles down the dell,
Though vanished now the pious hermit's cell.
And when we climb the summit of the hill
We find the same inviting prospect still,
Surrounding objects seeming ever new,
And Nature smiling in her fairest hue.
Brent Knoll is like old age: if but to heaven
Each passing year has been devoutly given,
Though shorn of dignity and robbed of grace,
Though bent the frame and wrinkled deep the face,
The happy prospect still the same appears,
Nay, gathers glory with revolving years!
Loved eminence! I mount thy breezy height
Each time I ramble with a fresh delight;
Yet oft that joy is mingled with a tear
When I recall the recollection dear

Of by-gone scenes and happy childhood's days,
When blithe I gambolled as yon lamb that plays;
Or, panting hard, thy slippery summit gained,
And, to complete the task, each muscle strained.
What now the view that greets my ravished gaze,
That all around Jehovah's power displays!
Which beauteous portion shall I earliest trace
Of these fair lineaments of Nature's face?
Mendip! thy lengthy range first meets mine eye,
Rising from far, then melting into sky:
Thy form at first a mountain's aspect wears,
Near where proud minster its high head uprears.
Wells is thy birthplace! with its thousand rills
Which bubble forth from all surrounding hills.
O sacred spot! so made by generous heaven,
Which to thy share has choicest blessings given,
Thy city like the fair Jerusalem—
Jehovah's dearest, richest, brightest gem—
Securely rests defended on each side
By mountain ramparts, that shall e'er abide,
When storms that rage and hurricanes that blow
Shall prostrate bastions and lay fences low,
Which art hath builded and which men have reared
Against the enemy whose force they feared;

Thy minster's honours who can duly raise,
Or give those holy walls their meed of praise?
Who shall describe her stately towers that rise
From firm foundations to eternal skies,
Or who shall count the various saints that grace
The gorgeous niches of her western face:
Who shall depict her storied windows true,
Bedight with colours of each rainbow hue?
Vain the attempt! beyond my feeble lyre—
I can but gaze, and wonder, and admire!
Proceed we now along proud Mendip's height,
Whose every feature fills us with delight,
Now naked, rocky, barren, sterile, bare,
Now richly carpeted with bracken fair,
Now without broom, or fern, or furze-bush clad,
Now made by flower and copse and heather glad.
Cheddar! thy chasm next arrests our eyes,
Thy towering rocks that high and heavenward rise,
Which seem to scorn the lowly plain of earth,
And upward mount towards Him who gave them birth.
Say! whose the hand yon great convulsion made,
That forced through Mendip's range that rocky glade,
Was it some current vast that urged its way
Through every barrier that before it lay?

Was it some earthquake with destructive might
That cleft the mountain from its topmost height?
Go, ask the Angel Host, the place that guard,
Nor seek an answer from an humble bard,
And they will tell thee in that solemn day
When sun withdrew and hid his face away,
When on the Cross the Lamb for sinners slain
Hung in His anguish and His dying pain;
When His lips, quivering in the pangs of death,
Uttered that shout which spent His latest breath,
These conscious rocks began to quiver too,
Burst from each other and exposed to view
The fertile country and the rugged shore,
Which, intercepting, they had hid before!
But other summits court a passing glance:
See yonder Peak, his pointed form advance,
Which seems to scorn a gaze on aught abroad,
And points us upward to fair Nature's God.
How oft I've clambered up yon rugged steep,
Though difficult the slippery path to keep,
When hoary frost has hung upon its brow,
And in huge flakes has fallen winter's snow;
Then in the stony rostrum I have stood,
And all around the beauteous prospect viewed;

Then mocked the orator's persuasive tongue,
And of each object in succession sung
To early friends and many a playmate dear,
Who deigned to listen and stood round to hear.
But pass we now through Shiplate's shady groves
Which seem in Mendip's bosom to repose,
Towards the wind-swept height of Bleadon Hill,
Which human hand has never toiled to till,
Though slumber here the ashes of the slain,
The Saxon victor and the vanquished Dane.
Bleadon! thy bracken forms the warrior's crest,
Marks out his tomb and blossoms o'er his breast,
And tells the traveller winding up the dell,
"'Twas here thine ancestor in battle fell!"
But, gracious audience! pardon if I stray,
Led by the Muse from Mendip's range away;
Or if abrupt I leave the towering height,
Since in the plain my home appears in sight!
The lagging courser, when his stall he nears,
Quickens his pace, his eager head uprears,
Lightly he steps along the well-known road,
When distant seen he eyes his loved abode,
Snuffing the breeze which softer seems to come,
Because 'tis wafted from the groves of home.

Then when yon steeple greets my longing eye,
With wingéd footsteps I towards it fly,
Faster than steel impelled by loadstone's force,
To that dear object I direct my course.
How oft in childhood, when compelled to leave
My own loved birthplace, would my bosom heave
With many a heavy sigh, and grief would start
Through every secret channel from my heart.
When to yon tower I've breathed a last adieu,
As rolling wheels along the turnpike flew;
How oft I've turned with trembling hand to dry
The scalding tear which gathered in mine eye:
And, oh, at length, when many a month has passed,
I've caught the longed-for minarets at last,
How have I hailed the soul-inspiring sight,
My spirit almost melting with delight!
And have these boyhood feelings disappeared?
Or like yon leaf, which autumn's hand hath seared,
Begin they now to wither and decay?
Not so, kind reader, gentle listener—nay,
If less enthusiastic now my love,
Time hath not, cannot, the affection move
That still I cherish for my native place,
While earlier haunts with eager step I trace.

No, never shall I catch thy tower from far,
By blaze of day, by twinkling light of star,
Without emotion kindling in my breast,
And thoughts of love and tenderness confessed.
Lympsham! to thee I'll consecrate my days,
Promote thine interest, raise thy lasting praise,
If one so humble can extend thy fame,
Or aught advance thy dearly lovéd name.
No sacred bay that grows on classic tree,
Which brings not grace, or good, or pride to thee,
Shall I e'er think it worth my while to gain,
Though within reach and easy to obtain;
Nor is there any which might haply tend
Thy peace, or joy, or glory to extend,
I would not strive to grasp with all my might,
Although it grew on labour's rocky height,
That, when secured, my proud reward might be,
To weave with it a verdant wreath for thee.
No happier prospect is before mine eyes,
No higher castle build I in the skies
Than in my birthplace all my days to spend,
The peasant's pastor and the poor man's friend.
Dearer to me the daisy of thy lea,
Thy woodbine wild, the haunt of many a bee,

Thy cowslip yellow and thy scarlet rose,
That on its leaf of green seems to repose,
Than loveliest flow'rets brought from foreign shores,
Which the delighted botanist explores:
Dearer to me thy circumscribéd lawn,
Sparkling with dew on summer morning's dawn,
Than boundless parks that stretch their wide domain
O'er hill and dale, and eminence and plain,
Where sportive deer and nimble stags do play
From morn till eve, and weary out the day:
Dearer to me thine honoured rectory!
With windows dight with Gothic tracery,
With pointed portico and crested towers,
Around whose bases blossom summer flowers,
Than all the lodges and the halls of state,
Where dwell the mighty and repose the great.
Dearer to me thine ancient steeple grey,
Raised by some pious hand some bygone day,
With massy buttresses and niches fair,
And towering pinnacles that pierce the air;
Than e'en proud Salisbury's spire, amazing sight,
Which rises upwards just four times the height:
Dearer to me thy churchyard, planted o'er
With dingy cypress and green sycamore,

With sable yew and weeping willows brave,
That droop their branches o'er some new-made grave:
Thy broken tombstones whose inscriptions traced
Time's ruthless hand hath nearly now effaced;
Than the proud sepulchres of potent kings,
Over whose ashes fame her dirges sings,
That rest in state within the groinèd aisle
Of ancient Westminster's distinguished pile;
And dearer, too, each honest rustic's face,
Who smiles, on passing, with a country grace,
Than aught 'twere possible for me to tell,
If tuned my lyre, though harped my fingers well.
Return we now to Mendip's range once more,
New scenes to contemplate and sights to explore;
And, passing Uphill's bleak and barren height,
Brean Down's bold outline will appear in sight,
Whose mighty rocks are lashed by Severn's waves,
Whose inmost caverns the proud breaker laves,
Dashing the silvery spray from side to side,
As in full grandeur swells the advancing tide.
How often on yon summit have I stood,
And the fair landscape stretched around me viewed;
Sometimes beheld the main convulsed with storm,
With billows rising in terrific form;

And sometimes eyed the undisturbed expanse
In which the rocks reflected seemed to dance.
Oft in yon mossy caverns I have stayed,
From hour to hour my homeward course delayed,
Till lengthening shadows and fast closing eve
Chid my delay and bade me take my leave.
Surely Mount Carmel, where the Seer of God
Held for a time his solitary abode,
Somewhat resembles this fair hill in form,
In situation drear; exposed to storm
Both mounts appear: each is a promontory,
Stretching its barrier towards a western sea;
And from Brean Down, as from famed Carmel's height,
There shone from far a solitary light,
In bygone centuries, when Gildas here
Led his ascetic life with heart sincere;
Whose bright example, like a beacon ray,
Chased brooding darkness and black mists away.
How often, like the prophet, Gildas toiled,
With vest ungirdled, and by clambering soiled,
Up the steep path of yonder rough ascent,
With eye upon the summit fixed intent;
And when at length the topmost turf he trod,
Away from nature up to nature's God,

How would he turn his heaven-glistening eye,
Lifted in transport upwards to the sky;
And then, descending from the height once more,
How would he pace along the sea-girt shore,
Enter the humble sanctuary of God,
And sound His power, His truth, His grace abroad,
To honest rustics who attentive stand;
Come at His bidding, go at His command.
In later years a second Gildas came,
And dear shall ever be his honoured name,
While memory sighs o'er many a bygone scene,
With him connected and the shores of Brean.
The time would fail me did I stop to tell
Of Burnham's lighthouse or its wondrous well.
At Quantock's beauteous range I next must glance,
Which borders on the channel's wide expanse,
Whose silver surface is bestudded o'er
With islets twain 'twixt this and t'other shore.
Quantock! thy summits have before been sung
In softer notes and with a sweeter tongue
Than I possess: e'en from this very place
Yeatman thy beauties often loved to trace;
Thy wood-clad slopes, now gilded by the beam
Of evening sun, a lovely contrast seem

To Mendip's sterile heights which mostly rise
In naked grandeur to the archéd skies;
As if in sooth great Nature's partial hand,
When weaving tapestry to deck our land,
Had spent on Quantock all her worsteds fair,
And left the canvas stretched o'er Mendip bare,
Except within the far secluded glade,
Where e'en for Mendip ornaments she made.
Rising beneath old Quantock's eastern ridge,
Where river's banks are joined by iron bridge,
Wrapt in the dingy smoke of many a fire,
Behold Bridgwater's elevated spire.
Here busy commerce leads her laden train
Of vessels proud, that plough the mighty main,
And bustles fast through every crowded street,
Like fabled Mercury with "wingéd feet."
But, leaving now a scene of constant change,
Observe we Polden's gently-rising range,
So called, perhaps, because in time of war,
From Polden's summit might be seen afar
The royal standard floating in the breeze,
High waving o'er the tops of neighbouring trees.
But farther south a fairer hill is seen,
Wrapt in a verdant vest of evergreen;

Few bards have ever dared to sing its praise
Since none could reach it with inferior lays;
For the same reason I, too, must be mute,
And only give its name "sweet Montacute!"
Mention we now but one fair summit more,
And that the far-famed Glastonbury Tor,
Where the last abbot suffered shameful death,
And into murderous hands resigned his breath.
'Twas here that many centuries before,
As those report who boast of ancient lore,
A holy visitor unlooked-for came,
Of birth illustrious and of noble name,
And planted firm on Glaston's height forlorn
The never-dying, because sacred, thorn.
No Christmas yet hath whitened Glaston's brow,
With its accompanying fall of snow,
That hath not witnessed this fair thorn in bloom,
Which blossomed first near Joseph's new-made tomb.
This precious relic I myself have seen,
And plucked from off its boughs a sprig of green,
For sake of him whose honoured name I bear,
That I with Glaston might the present share.
But closing evening bids me hush my lay,
With which I've wearied out a summer's day;

The sun descending sheds his latest beam,
Causing yon glittering vane afar to gleam,
And form, apparently, a crest of fire
Around the apex of yon lofty spire;
And now the orb has sunk his glowing head,
And in yon ocean made his tranquil bed;
And now the blue wave and the snowy spray
Steal all his glory, take his crown away;
Nor aught appears, save the last ray that steals
From lost Apollo's radiant chariot wheels.
Brent Knoll! accept a minstrel's parting tear:
Thy flowery summit shall be ever dear
To him, who with frail hand and faltering tongue
Thy loveliness has harped and feebly sung;
Who, now descending through the mossy dell,
Sighs forth to thee, blest mount, a sad farewell!

The Brean-down Cloud.*

LEEPING upon the lone hill side,
    The sombre shadow lay ;
  While all around the landscape wide
Smiled in the autumn ray.

I looked into the clear blue skies
    That shadow's cause to trace :
'Twas one fair cloud, to my surprise,
    Darkened the mountain's face.

On high, the fleecy mist was bright,
    Radiant in silver sheen ;
Below, the wreath of virgin-white
    In sable guise was seen.

---

* "As I was passing Brean-down on the rail, I saw a dark shadow resting on the bare side of the hill. Seeking its cause, I saw a little cloud, bright as light, floating in the clear blue above. Thus it is with our sorrow : it is dark and cheerless here on earth ; but look above and you see it to be but a shadow of His brightness whose name is Love."—*Extract from Dean Alford's Journal.—See Life,* p. 240.

And thus the chastisements of love
   Drop shadows as I go ;
But in yon azure vault above,
   Like noon-tide beams they glow.

Autumn.

After the manner of Scott.

AUTUMN yet lingers! Still the verdant spray
    Gleams in the coppice, midst the branches bare;
While through the watery cloud the struggling ray
   Flings o'er the forest-glade a lustre fair,
As if the waning year would proudly dare
   To vie in radiance with the summer sheen,
Charms of October vainly to compare,
   With August-glances through the tangled screen,
When in their pomp of power Apollo's steeds are seen!

Autumn yet lingers! Mendip's swelling breast,
   In richest purple royally arrayed,
No hour anticipates when soaring crest
   Shall 'neath a silvery veil of snow be laid;
When the sad shepherd, pensive and dismayed,
   Shall seek the covert of the sheltered vale,
Of chill December's angry blasts afraid,
   As howls Boreas with terrific wail,
Driving him home at last to tell the winter's tale.

Autumn yet lingers! and methinks its days,
   As years roll onward, seem more dear to me ;
I covet now no summer's gorgeous rays,
   No spring-tide blossoms, garnishing the lea.
Nay give me now the yellow half-stripped tree :
   I yield thee back gay bird and gayer flower :
Nature decaying sheds more sympathy :
   No more I ask for pleasure, pomp, or power ;
But only woo the spell that wakes in Autumn's hour.

The Firs have Fallen.

THE firs have fallen, and the Knoll looks in,
  Smiles recognition through the opened glade.
  Long have I loved both Knoll and fair domain ;
But they were sundered by the envious grove.
Now they are one ; and, both more beautiful,
Seem to rejoice that they each other know.
Thus have I brought together friends beloved ;
And never to our view has each appeared
So lovely, as at length, when both combined,
Have blessed each other, and the charm confessed
Our heart which ravished, when admiring both.

Buncombe Hill on a Summer's Evening.

NOT only in the distant North,
   Beyond the Pentlands and the Forth,
     Had he the landscape scanned;
Albion from shore to shore he knew,
From many a cairn had caught the view
     In Cambria's mountain land.

Had climbed dark Mona's summit lone,
Where erst King Orrey reared his throne
     In the enchanted isle;
While softer scenes 'twas his to trace,
Where southern seas in still embrace
     Round Norman islets smile.

But never was it his to see
Beneath wide heaven's high canopy
     A richer, goodlier land
Than he may view in summer bright
Who rests reclined on Quantock's height,
     Or doth on Willsneck stand.

Here hill and dale and timbered plain,
And cliff-bound shore and outstretched main
   Feast the admiring eye;
And modest towers rise here and there,
And manse, and cot, and homestead fair,
   Clustering around them lie.

If calm enjoyment you would find,
Repose for wearied frame and mind,
   Come to the favoured West;
With loving daughter wander free:
Not mountain moth, nor bird, nor bee
   Shall claim completer rest!

Greenaleigh.

MUTE on the spot the climber stood,
   And all around the landscape viewed,
     Ravished with glad surprise;
And praised the land that gave him birth,
As fairest in the bounds of earth,
   In his admiring eyes!

Beneath his feet old Minehead lay,
With pebbly beach and placid bay:
   And 'thwart the inland sea
Stretched Cambria, from Carmarthen's height,
To where the Wyndcliff meets the sight,
   Rising o'er Chepstow's lea.

Yonder rose Croydon's desert line:
Beneath, the blending braes combine,
   Behind him in the rear:
Brendon looks skyward overhead,
With purple garniture o'erspread;
   And Dunkery's crests appear.

Nor is there in the goodly whole
A gem more peerless than the knoll
   Where Conigar doth stand
Midst verdant bowers of tufted trees,
That still the battle and the breeze
   Defy on Luttrell's land!

O Somerset! my cherished home,
Ne'er from thy limits can I roam
   In search of scenes more fair;
Let others wander where they will,
I'll rest upon the western hill,
   In satisfaction there!

The Glastonbury Gathering.

JOSEPH a pilgrim from Mount Zion came,
    (So says the legend of the days gone by)
    Planting his staff, and leaving his fair name
To favoured Glaston's plain and hills on high.

No Christmas since has over Glaston flown,
    Leaving its snows on dale and upland spread,
When this famed wand hath not like Aaron's blown,
    And e'en in winter richest fragrance shed.

But greater annals have I lived to see,
    In later days when centuries have passed:
Within the year of Diamond Jubilee
    Have Church and Queen left memories long to last.

A hundred bishops in the ruined fane
    Have met, from North and South, and East and West,
To shew that common faith must ever reign
    'Mongst those in Christ in sweet communion blest.

Surely no fitter time could ever come,
   Our long-loved prelate's statue to display,
Whose dust reposes in the silent tomb,
   Whose ransomed spirit rests above for aye.

Long will Lord Arthur live in every heart
   That claimed his friendship whilst he lingered here;
And fondest memories can ne'er depart
   Till the blest Rising-morning shall appear.

Specially gracious to our favoured West
   Has "the Chief Shepherd" been, in bishops given:
Still with an ardent prelate are we blest,
   Succeeding him recalled from earth to heaven.

Early Snow in Autumn.

'TWAS an October Sabbath eve,
　　The groves and glades were green,
　And only here and there a leaf
　　Glimmered in golden sheen.

When back my window-blind I drew
　　Upon the Sabbath morn,
Lo there appeared before my view
　　A wintry waste forlorn !

For in the night the chilly skies
　　Had dropped their fleecy pall,
And now, to my profound surprise,
　　Cold snow had covered all.

Yes ! on the lawn, parterres, and trees,
　　The flakes of winter lay :
You might have thought the northern breeze
　　Had brought our Christmas-day.

Never before did I behold
   Snows in October lie :
Our parish patriarch—so I'm told—
   Astonished was as I.

As I surveyed the elms, still gay,
   Yet silver-mantled o'er,
The laurel bright, and glossy bay,
   Like winter's trophies—hoar ;

These were the thoughts that came to me
   Upon the Sabbath-day :—
I set them down right speedily,
   Lest they should pass away :—

Thus, when our life has reached its prime,
   Ere yet our leaves are sere,
Come change and death, before their time,
   With icy hand severe.

While all around is green and fair,
   The snow-cloud gathers high ;
And death descends in iron car
   From out the angry sky.

Prospects, and plans, and hopes, and schemes,
    Are prematurely riven;
And joys, like morn-dissolving dreams,
    By sudden griefs are driven.

I looked again. The scene was bright,
    Though hoar with winter's breath;
All sparkling in the Sabbath light,
    Too beautiful for death;

And as I gazed upon each spray,
    All clothed in silver snow,
Methought 'tis joy and life this day
    Portrays; not death and woe.

A vision then before me smiled
    Of Christ's return from heaven;
When robes of whiteness, undefiled,
    Shall to His Church be given.

Some shall be living on that night,
    All green, like yonder grove:
Then shall descend the virgin light,
    All spotless, from above;

And " clothed upon " each living tree
   In purity shall shine,
Life melt in immortality,
   At Jesu's glance divine.

Easter Even, April 11, 1857.

A day of howling storm, occasional showers, and warm sunshine combined.

THE darkling cloud is overhead,
    The storm comes howling by;
Anon the golden beams are shed,
    And smiles the deep blue sky.

Sure nature brings her sympathy
    To Revelation's shrine;
Responsive thrills with Calvary,
    Where sun and storm combine.

That howling blast in echo spoke
    Stern Justice's behest;
Then melting Mercy gently woke
    In sunbeam, and caressed!

Those heavy drops are Sion's tears
    On Golgotha that fell;
But pardon in those tints appears
    Which in yon rainbow dwell.

Dear April and sweet Eastertide,
   Ye meetly come together :
Our dying Lord would thus provide
   A preacher in the weather !

Christmas.

HAIL sacred festival! I haste to-day
   To greet thine advent with a rustic lay.
     Ye angels, tune my lyre,
While I with willing fingers sweep
Those chords that bid me smile and weep,
   As I to sing aspire.

Since Constantine the Roman throne
Climbed but to make the world his own,
   And scatter heaven's pure light,
Albion has greeted Bethlehem's star,
Around her coasts, or near or far,
   Beaming with radiance bright.

Each rolling age some tribute brings,
Some offering to the King of kings,
   As did the seers of old;
When frankincense with myrrh entwined,
Their varying hues and scents combined,
   With gifts of Eastern gold.

In earlier times the festal board,
Encircled by the serf and lord,
 The ample hall displayed ;
While youth and age rejoiced in pairs,
Both auburn locks and hoary hairs,
 The matron and the maid.

Turkey, and goose, and capon fair,
Furnished the festival so rare,
 And brave old oxen fell ;
And toast-brown'd ale and wassail bowl,
From host to guest stirred every soul,
 Prompting grim tales to tell.

Holly, and mistletoe, and yew,
Hung round as thick as if they grew
 Forth from the 'scutcheoned wall ;
And brave yule log its lustre shed,
Blazing from out its ashy bed
 Along the ancient hall.

And carol-band before the gate,
With brightened eye and heart elate,
 Advance for Christmas cheer ;

And sing of shepherds' watch by night,
When lustrous beams of heavenly light
　　Kindled both hope and fear.

Forth from the ivied tower hard by
Rose the loud peal's rich melody,
　　Borne on the midnight breeze ;
While winter o'er the churchyard hung,
And cold his snowy mantle flung
　　O'er tombstones, graves, and trees.

Sober the garb religion wore,
Sincere yet sober thoughts of yore
　　Rose in the churchman's breast ;
Then holy hymns for "Church and King !"
And sacred carols, would men sing
　　Ere came the hour of rest.

Meek deference then her charm would weave,
And lowliness her curtsey give,
　　With mute and blushing grace ;
Ere liberalism's fatal spell
Scorched as with blasting flames of hell
　　The present century's face.

O fair and happy days gone by,
When Albion's aristocracy
  Graced well their feudal halls!
And banner waved from dungeon keep,
And turrets frowned from craggy steep
  Along the lichened walls.

Yet up and down in England yet
There linger those who would forget
  The spirit of the day;
Old tory hearts that still would sing
Their "three-times-three for Church and King!"
  From eve to morning ray.

If on your rounds you chance to light
On such a true-born ancient wight,
  Bid him to Lympsham come;
Essay our door on Christmas-eve,
When jovial welcomes we will give—
  Make such a guest at home.

Still shall he see the yule log glow,
All blazing on the hearth below,
  Still taste the Christmas cheer,

Still see the berried holly smile,
Still with gay song the gloom beguile
   That waits the changing year!

Hurrah once more for Church and King
Ye lads and lasses each one sing!
   The altar and the throne;
"What God hath joined let none divide:"
He can be nought but parricide
   Who would our Church disown!

May fair Victoria's latest days
Be crowned with amaranthine bays,
   Peace, plenty, and renown;
And love, and loyalty, and truth,
Refresh our age, adorn our youth,
   And on our babes look down.

Pleasure and Duty.

'TWAS a fine summer morning, and bright shone the sun,
As forth from the mountains his race he begun;
Miss Pleasure passed by me, all radiant in glee,
And gaily invited, " Come trip it with me!"

So away we both rambled all through the green wood,
While plucking the flowerets to twine in her snood;
And the ring of her laughter was merry and gay,
As blithe as the brooklet that danced in our way.

Yet the sun had scarce climbed to his throne in the sky,
Ere her smiles were all darkened and sullen her eye;
And while I was musing the reason to trace,
She turned round and gave me a slap in the face.

'Twas a bleak winter dawning, and driftings of rain
Rattled rudely in gusts on the dark window pane;
Dame Duty awoke me, as sternly she said,
" Thy slumbers are over, arise from thy bed!"

So away we set forth on the round of the day,
The wild winds were out o'er the snow as it lay;
While sternly she wended her course up the hill,
And as we ascended walked moody and still.

Yet, when we had climbed it, so pleasant she grew,
That, says I to myself, "What! can it be you?"
And when I looked next on the face of my guide,
Methought 'twas an angel that walked at my side!

I Pace the Ocean's Rugged Shore.

I PACE the ocean's rugged shore,
And listen while its billows roar ;
And wide across their crested foam
My far-stretched eye delights to roam ;
And written on the boundless sea,
I read my God's Infinity.

I climb at morn the heathery glen,
Apart from haunts of busy men ;
And 'neath the soaring mountain's breast
I watch the cloud that crowns his crest ;
Half veiled within the silent sky,
I read, my God, Thy majesty !

I wander through the cultured plain,
And mark the heavy-laden wain ;
And number o'er the shocks of corn,
And flocks which sunny slopes adorn ;
And ere the river meets the flood,
I hear it sing " My God is good ! "

I steal within the sylvan bower,
And breathe the fragrance of the flower
That wastes its odours on the air,
Displays unseen its colours rare;
Soft breezes through the coppice rove,
And whisper that my "God is love!"

And is it thus, O Lord, to me
Thy works are witnesses of Thee;
And sea, and mountain, field, and flower,
Proclaim thy wisdom, love, and power?
What must it be in heaven to trace,
And see without a veil Thy face!

Falling Bells.

THE music of the falling chime
   Recalls each scene of by-gone time—
   Now eddying swell, now sinking sound,
Thrilling the soul in rolling round.

Ye tuneful six, from steeple grey,
Have gladdened my sad heart to-day;
And woke once more that deeper joy
That seems refined from earth's alloy.

O tell me, wise Philosophy,
Why droops the heart 'midst revelry;
But ofttimes, 'midst surroundings sad,
Why is the soul so deeply glad?

The mystery wouldst thou seek to know?
So is it ordered here below:
No star can shed its mystic light
Till darkness shrouds the skies with night.

The hurricane the earth must shake
Ere yet "the still small voice" can wake:
If heaven's bright arch its tints would twine,
On the black cloud the bow must shine.

No spring-tide flowers can deck the spray
Till winter drear has held its sway:
Birds from that bush their lays must pour
Where icicles have hung before.

The snowdrop blossoms by the way
Where long the frozen snow-drift lay:
Descending rains must sweep the fell
That brooks may warble down the dell.

This, after all, the cause may be,
Not yet from bondage is earth free;
"The creature" waits for that blest hour
That vanquishes corruption's power.

Then cloudless skies shall gild the span
That arches o'er redeemèd man;
Deep seas of bliss rise swelling o'er,
Without a shallow or a shore.

Rich melodies around shall float,
Unmingled with a minor note;
While quenchless suns that never set
Shall bathe each golden minaret,

And flash from out each sparkling stone
That garnishes the City's zone,
And lustre lends to that deep flood
That girds the paradise of God.

O Jesu! through that pearly gate
May I, Thy servant, wend and wait;
And, ransomed by Thy blood alone,
Wonder and worship at Thy throne!

Wordsworth's Grave.*

THOU slumberest not near royal dust,
    With many a kindred bard :
    The village churchyard claims the trust
Thy cherished form to guard.

And meet it is that thou shouldst rest,
    Just where they laid thee down ;
Till the Archangel comes in quest
    Of those he seeks to crown.

The mountains watch thy lowly grave,
    The brooklet murmurs near,
The thorn and yew tree o'er thee wave,
    Drop evening dews their tear.

Right fitly chosen are the trees
    That grace thy modest mound,

---

* The grave of the poet Wordsworth lies in the south-east corner of Grasmere Churchyard, together with those of his family, and that of Hartley Coleridge. It has a thorn on one side and a yew tree on the other. The stream brawls below, beyond the churchyard wall.

That softly sigh when evening breeze
   Whispers through hallowed ground.

The thorn—it meekly seems to say,
   " Life's thorns disturb not now ;
My Saviour took them all away,
   And wreathed them round His brow."

The mystic everlasting yew,
   Proclaims that thou shalt rise ;
And, budding like itself anew,
   Shalt flourish in the skies.

Wordsworth ! thy memory's more dear,
   Since to thy vale I came,
Where many a rustic sheds the tear,
   And smiles to hear thy name.

They knew thee, and they loved thee well,
   And love to speak of thee,
And gladly will they to me tell
   Of how thou used to be.

How thou didst walk these lonely fells,
   And climb these living heights,

And in their solitary dells
　Enjoy thine own delights.

And how men met thee in the grove,
　Or by the mountain force,
And heard the poet of their love
　Unto himself discourse.

For ofttimes thoughts would language claim,
　All welling from within,
Thoughts that so wild and vivid came,
　Thou couldst not keep them in.

Men heard thee "muttering on thy way,"*
　With earnest head bowed down;
Nor guessed they what they heard thee say
　Was winning thy renown;

That holy poesy from thee
　Would to the world be given,
To teach to men truth's mystery,
　To guide their steps to heaven.

* This was the description given me of the poet by the Cumbrians themselves. They said, "You could hear Mr. Wordsworth muttering to himself a long time before he came up to you."

Songs of Somerset.

E'en while I weave this simple lay,
    Dear Wordsworth, o'er thy tomb,
Full many a pilgrim on this day
    Like to myself doth come

To write thy brief memorial down,
    To shed the silent tear
O'er virtue, truth, and just renown
    That crowned our laureate's bier!

Songs of Somerset.

The Bee Hive.

BLEADON, Burnham, Berrow, Brent,
Sir, your bees will all be spent!
Nay, Sir, we have several more,—
Badgworth, Biddisham, yet in store,
Blagdon, Bridgwater, and Brean,
Stock our bee-hive full, I ween.

Appendix.

Appendix.

Note I.

WILLETT TOR rises on the property of the late J. Blommart, Esq. It is an outlier of the Brendon range, and commands a rich prospect of all that lovely part of the country between the Quantock and the Brendon hills. I visited it first on a day peculiarly favourable to the tourist—in the spring of 1853,—when the surrounding woods were bright in their early freshness.

Note II.

"DUNKERY" is a lofty mountain lying about eight miles south from Minehead. From the church at Wootton Courtenay, the ascent to its summit is three miles. Its altitude is estimated at about seventeen hundred feet above the level of the sea. It is covered almost entirely with heather, intermixed with the whortleberry plant, and some rare bog and other mosses. On a clear day "the view," from the Beacon, says Mr. Savage, in his *History of the Hundred of Carhampton*, "extends on the south-west to the high lands near Plymouth; and on the north to the Malvern Hills in Worcestershire; two parts of the country which are more than two hundred miles distant from each other. On the west and north-west, the Bristol Channel, for nearly one-hundred-and-thirty miles in length, lies under the eye, with the greater part of South Wales, from Monmouthshire down to Pembrokeshire, rising in a fine ampitheatre beyond it. To the east and south the greater part of Somersetshire, Dorset, and Devon, with some parts of Hants and Wilts, appear in view. When the air is clear and not too bright, the line which bounds the horizon cannot be less than five hundred miles in circumference, circumscribing fifteen counties. On the top of Dunkery there is a vast collection of rough loose stones, from one pound to two hundred pounds in weight each; and among them the ruins of three large fire-hearths, about eight feet square, and built of rough unhewn stones. These fireplaces form an equilateral triangle, and in the centre there is another hearth considerably larger than the rest. . . . . . . These are the remains of those beacons which were formerly erected on this elevated spot, in order to alarm the country in times of civil discord or foreign invasion. Hence, the highest point of this hill is called Dunkery Beacon. To the north, south, and east of the ridge on which the Beacon stands, the mountain slopes down for a long distance; but on the western side it joins the high lands which connect it with the Forest of Exmoor. . . .

Appendix.

The Beacon is often covered with clouds, and then becomes a stupendous local barometer; for on such occasions rain is certain speedily to follow."—(Savage's *History of the Hundred of Carhampton*, pp. 5, 7.)

Note III.

THIS fragment describes a walk with a friend from Porlock Weir to the romantic village of Culbone, after we had spent the morning on Dunkery. The situation of the hamlet is thus described by the Rev. R. Warner, of Bath, in his *Walk through some of the Western Counties of England:* "A small cove of an oval form opened upon us, the bottom of which is formed by a little verdant carpet of two or three acres. Around this hollow the hills, on every side save on that which is next the sea, tower up in a direction nearly perpendicular, to the sublime height of twelve or thirteen hundred feet, fretted with jutting rocks and laden with venerable woods. Here the oak's solemn shade is relieved by the bright berry of the mountain ash; and there the light satin of the airy birch is chastened by the gloom of the melancholy yew, whilst the feathering fir and the luxuriant beech lend their contrasting foliage to give a wider variety to the enchanting scene. At the mouth of the cove, the land suddenly falls to the shore in an abrupt descent of four or five hundred feet, rough with enormous crags and stones, but enlivened with verdure and foliage quite to the beach. In the centre of the little recess thus surrounded and defended from the intrusion of the stranger, stands the lilliputian church of Culbone, a gothic structure, thirty-three feet in length and twelve in breadth, with a cemetery of proportionate dimensions stretching around it, appropriately ornamented with broken modest gravestones, and the remains of an ancient stone cross. Two cottages, planted just without the consecrated ground, are its only companions in this secluded dell."—(See Warner's *Walk through some of the Western Counties of England*, pp. 94, 95).

The scene opens with a description of Porlock Weir, with Lord Lovelace's beautiful grounds adjoining, through which the path leads to Culbone.

Note IV.

THE range of Quantock (Celtic *Gwantog*, *i.e.*, abounding in openings), is about fifteen miles in length by four in breadth, extending from North Petherton and West Monkton on the east, to Quantoxhead and St. Audries on the west. Its highest summits are Cothelstone, Willsneck, and Danesborough, the loftiest of which (Willsneck) reaches an altitude of nearly thirteen hundred feet above the level of the sea. From Willsneck, particularly, the prospect is exceedingly rich and extensive. On the south stretches the Vale of Taunton Deane, clad in the most luxuriant foliage of elm, beech, and oak, studded with villages and fair churches, and bounded by the

Appendix.

blue line of Blagdon, on which the Wellington column stands boldly prominent. Towards the east, you have a number of inferior summits, amongst which the triple knolls of Montacute, wrapped in their vest of evergreen, are very conspicuous. Beyond these the eye wanders towards the more distant heights of Frome and Warminster, till the bleak wolds of Dorset bound the horizon. Northward, you have the indented coast of Wales, separated by the intervening Channel, with its two rocky islets of Flat and Steep Holm, the bold promontories of Brean Down and St. Thomas's Head, Crook's Peak, Cheddar, and the whole Mendip range, in the undulations of which may be glimpsed at intervals the line of Wraxall Down stretching behind, till it terminates in the misty point of Portishead. Turning to the west, a sea of miniature mountains meets the climber's gaze; Willett, Brendon, Treborough, and Nettlecombe, with old Dunkery in the background, tossing up its heathy head, a very mountain-monarch, to the height of over seventeen hundred feet above the waters of Porlock Bay, of which he stands the guardian, and who, with his Exmoor brethren, terminates the landscape; all beyond being dim cloud and misty vapour. But the glory of Quantock is, after all, its almost countless combes—towards the east more luxuriant and richly wooded—towards the west wilder and more majestic in their character, with " heath and fern all waving wide," and " cold greystone " darting up at intervals amidst the tufted grass. In wandering along the soft silvery stream banks by which Cockercombe and Sevenwells combe are watered, you might fancy yourself nearing "Loch-Katrine" and "Ellen's Isle." In climbing Bicknoller Gorge, carpeted with mountain fern for some eight hundred feet above you, till the purple heather brightens into a blushing border higher up, a very slight stretch of imagination would fix you in "Rob Roy's country," or the wilder Highlands.

Printed and published by Barnicott and Pearce,
at the Athenaeum Press, Taunton.
mdcccxcviii

www.ingramcontent.com/pod-product-compliance
Lightning Source LLC
Chambersburg PA
CBHW020109170426
43199CB00009B/458